PRESERVING the CHESAPEAKE BAY

LESSONS IN THE POLITICAL REALITY
OF NATURAL RESOURCE STEWARDSHIP

Based on remarks by
The Honorable Gerald L. Baliles
former Governor of Virginia, to the McLain Program in
Environmental Studies at Washington College in Chestertown, MD

Publication was made possible by generous grants from Chesapeake Corporation,
Norfolk Southern Corporation and Westvaco Corporation.

Published by the Virginia Museum of Natural History Foundation, Martinsville, VA.

Proceeds will benefit the Virginia Museum of Natural History and
the Chesapeake Bay Foundation.

To that end, John Barber contributed selected paintings from his remarkable
works on the Chesapeake Bay to illustrate text.

Similarly, John Hurt Whitehead III of Urbanna, publisher of
Watermen of the Chesapeake Bay, donated his photographs to bring the text to life.

Mark Smith, a Richmond graphic designer who lives in Urbanna,
designed Preserving the Chesapeake Bay.

FOREWORD BY JOHN W. DANIEL II

Known internationally as one of the world's most unique and significant estuaries, the Chesapeake Bay has declined in its once prolific production of oysters and crabs. Today, its future depends on the endeavors of a cadre of allies who are often perceived as unlikely collaborators. Its restoration is not led by a single constituency. It solicits the participation of all of us. From boardrooms to brown bag lunches, the goals and the dreams of tomorrow's Chesapeake Bay are universal. And therein lies the basis for success.

Unlike so many facets of the natural resource trust, the Chesapeake Bay provides tangible interest on our investment. Dividends are in direct proportion to both human and financial expenditure. The scientific community measures quantitative improvement in water quality, the restoration of aquatic species and invigorated habitat. The recreational enthusiast witnesses firsthand the resurgence of waterfowl, the presence of brown pelicans and bald eagles, and the return of striped bass. Business and industry appreciate the importance of the Chesapeake for commerce. Residents—full and part-time—know the importance of the Bay as a retreat. The environmental community is vigilant to point out the necessity of maintaining our course for greater success.

Continued depletion of habitat, both wetlands and submerged aquatic vegetation, directly impacts the production and vitality of our seafood industry. Chesapeake Bay oysters, once the calling card of our great Commonwealth, have virtually disappeared. Certain species of fish decline at alarming rates. Inattentive development creates negative impacts on water quality that threaten the habitat of the Bay, home to thousands of species. And individuals sometimes fail to appreciate the impact on the Bay of their activities miles and miles away.

The Chesapeake Bay demonstrates its stamina by responding to our initiatives. The Bay compels us to use our very best judgment and wisdom to restore the estuary. For two decades, we have responded in a united and positive way to the call of the Bay. We have done so perhaps because we are all stakeholders, but more likely because it is a challenge that all can readily appreciate and a result that can easily be envisioned. The progress towards a healthy and vital Bay could not have taken place without the united approach and commitment of thousands of people. Progress has occurred, and will continue to occur, because the Chesapeake Bay helps us all to appreciate the importance of marshaling energy and resources to an achievable and defined set of goals.

People from across all socioeconomic spectra have contributed to revitalizing the Chesapeake Bay. They have done so as the result of self-imposed voluntary restrictions and in response to governmental calls for action. Without the hugely successful voluntary "best-management practices" undertaken by the forest industry, without the many volunteers who regularly hold "Clean the Bay" days, without "catch and release" programs sponsored by recreational users, and without literally hundreds of similar voluntary efforts, the Chesapeake would decline.

Similarly, the governmental role in the restoration of the Chesapeake has been significant. Whether through multi-state compacts, required demands for wastewater treatment, regulatory programs to control run-on and runoff, protection of important habitat and wetlands, or land use controls, such as Virginia's Chesapeake Bay Preservation Act, the willingness to couple these types of programs with the multitude of voluntary programs has historically been overwhelming.

A shared vision for the Chesapeake Bay by the numerous and varied constituencies who have contributed to the development of voluntary programs and who have sacrificed to fulfill their regulatory responsibilities has resulted in an alliance unparalleled in resource management. Chesapeake Bay programs are a model for overcoming difficult and often conflicting points of view. Throughout our mutual efforts, divergent points of view have sustained one another. Appreciation and latitude have been extended as the health of the Chesapeake Bay has been improved. The process has worked and the natural resource trust is the beneficiary.

The text that follows reminds us of those partnerships. It reminds us of the individual, corporate and governmental commitments. It sustains us by reminding us of how we are meeting the challenge. And it provides additional catalyst for an improved Chesapeake Bay by noting our accomplishments. Pictorially, we are shown the vision and are reminded of the importance of the task, the role we each must play, and the simplicity and complexity of a healthy and vibrant Chesapeake Bay.

I would be remiss if I did not note my personal gratitude to the author for his understanding and appreciation of the Chesapeake Bay, as well as Virginia's many special natural resources. His leadership and personal commitment helped many to become better stewards. I am fortunate to count myself among them.

John Daniel, the first Secretary of Natural Resources for Virginia, was the principal author of the 1987 Chesapeake Bay Agreement. He is a partner with McGuire, Woods, Battle & Booth, LLP

Why is the Bay important?   Why should we worry about keeping it clean?

First, its size alone commands attention. The Bay's watershed covers over 64 thousand square miles. This includes all the rivers, creeks and backyard streams that eventually drain into the Bay itself. This watershed stretches as far north as the Baseball Hall of Fame in Cooperstown, New York. It runs east to the first state, Delaware, and extends westward to the Appalachians of "wild, wonderful West Virginia." • And, even while accounting for its size, it is remarkably productive, both in environmental — and economic terms. The Bay's shallow depth allows flora and fauna dependent upon light to flourish in most of its waters. The Bay's complex currents, generated by its mix of fresh and salt water, amplify natural recycling processes, allowing the Bay to get the most out of available nutrients. • The Bay's Atlantic access draws back sea life from the ocean for spawning. The watershed's shorelines provide fertile soil for farming. This exceptional productivity makes the Bay commercially important to people worldwide. As a source of seafood alone, its numbers are impressive: 90% of the nation's soft-shell crab catch comes from the Bay; 55% of the country's blue crab harvest originates in the Chesapeake; and, before the growing impact of people interfered, the Chesapeake Bay served as the spawning ground for 90% of the striped bass along America's entire Atlantic Coast. • All told, the Bay's annual seafood catch totals 100 million pounds, with a dockside value in the tens of millions. So, from restaurants serving soft-shell crabs in Tokyo, to sunburned watermen of the Eastern Shore, to charter boat fishermen of the Atlantic, the Bay's commercial importance can be felt. These numbers don't even include the Bay's economic and social value, both as an avenue of transportation and a source of recreation. • Two of the world's busiest ports, Baltimore and Hampton Roads, lie on the Chesapeake's shores. Billions of dollars worth of imports and exports flow annually through the Bay's channels. And many other shoreline cities and towns harbor thousands of smaller

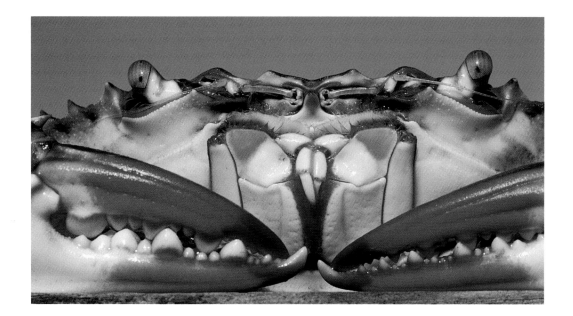

commercial and recreational boats. Dockyard workers and weekend sailors all depend on the

Chesapeake Bay, whether for their incomes or their peace of mind. • But we still have only

looked at the Bay's value to the human race. The Chesapeake's rivers and streams, wetlands and

beaches, inlets and channels, are vitally important as a home to wildlife. But, we humans cannot

accurately quantify <u>this</u> value of the Bay. This is just one root of the watershed's current

problems. With so many dependent upon the Bay for their incomes, or their lives, conflict over

the best use of the Chesapeake's resources has inevitably developed. Choices must be made.

• Let me briefly outline what we do know about the Chesapeake's problems and their causes.

One of the Bay's biggest problems might be categorized as "too much of a good thing." Fertilizer

runoff from croplands, nutrients from treated sewage and erosion from once-forested shorelines,

all contribute to a "nutrient overload." To make matters worse, the Chesapeake's exceptionally effective natural recycling ability compounds the effects of this nutrient glut. In short, the Bay

has too much food. • But why is so much food dangerous? This extra food has fueled an

explosion in the microscopic plant life dwelling in the Bay. These organisms block sunlight and

deplete the Chesapeake's waters of oxygen, making survival difficult for many other species.

Continuous harvesting of oysters has exacerbated the effects of the "bloom" of microscopic plant

life. • Before settling in one place, young oysters drift through the water, munching on the

microscopic life now in abundance, filtering the Bay as a result. Before 1870, the Bay held enough

oysters to filter all the water in the Chesapeake basin in only a few days. But now, with oyster

stocks depleted to just 1% of their 19th century levels, "filtration time" has inflated to one year. •

Oysters aren't the only victims. Unthinking harvesting and exploding land development have cut

the populations of other important watershed resources. Almost half the shores' forests and

wetlands have been cleared, drained or filled to handle the growing human population of

thousands upon thousands of people who annually move into this part of the country. Dams now

block streams that once served as spawning grounds for ocean-going, and freshwater fish,

amputating the Chesapeake from its tributaries. Plant and animal life that once called these areas

home have been displaced. And, until recently, few have cared where they might go next.

• Furthermore, forests and wetlands serve as an important buffer, trapping excess nutrients and

sediments in run-off. When you drain a wetland, or clear a shoreline forest, you deprive the Bay

of its natural protection against the nutrient overload from which it now suffers. The Bay is

stripped of its natural resilience against development's encroachment. This leaves the Bay hard

pressed to handle the mounting demands a growing human population has placed upon it. • It's

clear that the severely distressed condition of the Bay has been well documented. Abuse, neglect

nd lack of adequate care are the causes. In short, we've been overloading the Bay with nutrients,

ediments and dangerous chemicals, poisoning the water in the Bay bottom with toxic pollutants,

nd destroying wetlands and grasses which are key ingredients necessary for a healthy and

productive Bay. • One of my favorite quotes on the Chesapeake Bay compares the Bay of today

with yesterday's. "I've sailed the Chesapeake Bay...for half a century," writes Gil Grosvenor, a

riend of mine who is president and chairman of the National Geographic Society. He goes on to

ay: "With its rich melding of forest, field, water and sky, the Chesapeake has always represented

o me the best of this nation's outdoor heritage. Considering the wealth of its waters, the

productivity of its tilled fields, and the collection of industry along its shores, it has seemed a

microcosm of the developing world." • But then, he writes how the Chesapeake has changed

from the one he once knew. "Increasingly, the shoreline and creeks are sprouting clusters of

condominiums, the wetlands that drew hundreds of thousands of ducks and Canada geese each fall are being drained, bulldozed, and built over. I don't encourage my young son to swim in [the Bay], as I once did myself." He concludes: "The Bay is a microcosm all right, of what we have become, what we must correct, and what we have to avoid in the future." • It also provides a microcosm of the political and policy problems faced by government leaders today. And more importantly, the challenges over the last decade in shaping a series of Chesapeake Bay agreements signed by Maryland, Virginia, Pennsylvania, the District of Columbia, and the federal Environmental Protection Agency provide a model for considering the policy problems of tomorrow. • Initially, demands placed by a society upon government are simple. The quest for food, shelter, and clothing command the attention of a country's population — until those needs are met. But once these essentials for survival are secured, attention can be focused elsewhere

- Awareness of the outside world increases as people have more time to sample its offerings.

Clean water and air or expanded recreational facilities hold more importance in affluent regions. Beggars in India or migrant workers in South America will not take time to concern themselves with the threat of global warming if they are hungry as they go to sleep each night. But a plumber with a 40-hour work week and a comfortable income might notice he can't catch quite as many fish on his weekend boating trips as he once did. • In this regard, the United States has a two or three decade jump on other nations in the world. In Asia, Eastern Europe, Central and South America and other industrializing regions of the world, environmental awareness is in its early stages. These countries are just beginning to develop environmental regulations and controls and to factor environmental costs into choices made in public policy. • Meanwhile, the consequences of industrial development, expansion of transportation and construction upon our natural resources have been publicly debated for decades in America. • Both federal and state

governments have developed substantial administrative and regulatory resources to protect the

environment. But that doesn't mean we could have just flipped a switch to save the Bay. The

policy problems involved are much more complex, costly and time consuming. • It may seem

relatively simple to regulate or remove the obvious sources of pollution. It is not quite that easy.

Remember the size of the Bay and the scale of human activity, the movement of millions of people

within the Bay area, and the millions of people moving to the Bay region. All that activity creates

demands for new housing, new employment, better transportation, more recreational

opportunities — just to mention a few of the human activities that go on within the region.

• In addition, there are different levels of government — federal, state and local — that must be

considered. A decision today to take a pollution control step, in many cases, will require an

analysis of how to control a particular problem, then the design of control technology must be

done by a professional firm. When approved, the equipment must be ordered and, in many cases

built, all of which requires time. It must then be transported to the site for installation, which is

followed by a start-up period and monitoring to ensure compliance. • If the source of the

pollution problem is corporate, funds for expenditures must be found and approved by a board of

directors. If it is a public source, the level of government must raise the funds and allocate them

from tax revenues available. • If the problem is not controlled adequately by legislation, then

the appropriate level of government must develop proposed legislation, provide opportunities for

public hearing and debate before passage and implementation. • In the middle of all this, the

proposal often must compete with other demands for time, money and attention. Time is

required. Money must be found. Balances must be struck. • As we know in Maryland and Virginia,

state and local governments are required to operate with balanced budgets, but revenues are

shrinking relative to expenses. Furthermore, many political leaders have made policy decisions

not to raise taxes. Many people argue that tax increases during a recession only worsen the

effects of an economic downturn. This leaves only the choice of cutting services. Which services

get priority? • Education, mental health, transportation, law enforcement, economic

development and the environment are all important. And, in an ideal world, Maryland and

Virginia could spend as much as necessary on each. • Yet, fiscal constraints prevent this; and

some, or all, of the programs in these areas must be reduced or eliminated so that government

leaders can meet their fiduciary responsibilities. Those are not easy decisions to make; they are

not always understood or accepted. • Projecting worth has always been particularly ticklish with

environmental issues. The complexities of an ecosystem such as the Bay make quantitative

measurement of the effects of policy options difficult. The time required for results can make

political support sometimes difficult. • So, what do we do about this remarkable resource — the

Chesapeake Bay — which is fundamental to our economy, to our culture, to the very well being of

our lives? Stated another way, the questions are: what do we do about it? How do we respond?

• First, we have to discern the character of the damage done. And, thanks to the tenacity of one

Charles Mathias, former U.S. Senator from Maryland, the U.S. Environmental Protection Agency

won the Congressional support it needed some years ago to proceed with an historic seven-year

study to determine the status of the Bay's health. The picture was not pretty. Something needed

to be done — and done quickly. • The jurisdictions of the Chesapeake Bay region acted — by

forming a unique pact. It has been more than a decade now since December 1983 when the mayor

of Washington, the governors of Virginia, Maryland, Pennsylvania, and the administrator of EPA affixed their signatures to the historic Chesapeake Bay Agreement and pledged the mutual

support of the jurisdictions to do what was necessary. It was, understandably, quite general, a

pledge to cooperate, to begin the journey to clean up the Bay. • Of course there was initial

skepticism. It was said the states and the District of Columbia could not effectively work together,

that they would not put their money where their mouths were, that the federal government

would not put its money on the line. But the jurisdictions began by acknowledging that the

decades old decline of the Bay would not be turned around overnight. Commitments were made

to the long haul, to pooling resources, energies and talents into an unrelenting effort. Plans were

developed, funds were committed. While quite general in nature, what's important is this: the

signers of that first agreement put in place a process — one which would advance in stages the

determined pursuit of the Bay's restoration. • In 1987 in my second year as governor of Virginia,

I became chairman of the Chesapeake Bay Executive Council, the regional group created by that

pact. Based upon my review of the progress made and the enormous challenges remaining, I

urged that the time was right to expand our frame of reference, to broaden our focus beyond the

general issues of environmental quality and data gathering to specific goals and benchmarks of

pollution prevention, species protection, habitat restoration and fisheries management. • We

agreed that we must design a monitoring system that would enable us to measure clearly and

precisely our rate of success in cleaning the Bay; a system that would publicly demonstrate the

progress, one that would involve more effective partnerships between states and local

governments, between all governments and private interests, and between government and the

people themselves. It seemed to be crucial that the public understand the ends of the Chesapeake

Bay effort in order that we could continue to build the support needed for political and financial resources. • It also seemed to me that it was critical that we construct a process that would last beyond our terms in office. So I requested and received reports from citizens advisory committees, local government committees, and scientific and technical advisory committees on their proposals for a new Chesapeake Bay agreement. Based on their advice we convened a drafting committee to use those recommendations as the foundation for a new agreement. We then convened a Chesapeake Bay Summit in Norfolk in August of 1987. The governors, mayor and the EPA administrator hammered out an agreement over several days and then released the draft agreement to the public and the press. During the following three or four months, we reviewed all public comments and incorporated them, where appropriate, into a final version which we signed in Baltimore with Governor Schaefer as host in December 1987. It was a remarkable effort that not only formed the basis for more specific action to clean up the Bay, but laid down the

foundation for the third agreement signed in 1992 in Washington. That agreement continued to build upon the process of commitments made during the last decade with even more specific goals and programs. • It is impossible to describe the details of that important 1987 Chesapeake Bay Agreement. It is important to understand that it was divided into a series of eight specific goals and 29 related commitments. Let me briefly mention just three of the areas of the agreement. (1) Living Resources. The ultimate measure of the Chesapeake Bay's health is its living productivity. The agreement contained a section on living resources with specific timetables for the development and adoption of specific criteria for the protection of habitat conditions and developing Bay-wide fisheries management plans for commercial and recreational species. The agreement called for the development of such schedules within six months to a year and those deadlines were met. (2) Water Quality. The improvement and maintenance of water

quality is the single most critical element in the overall restoration and protection of the

Chesapeake Bay. We agreed to adopt specific programs such as developing by July 1988 a basin-

wide plan to reduce nutrients entering the Bay system by 40% by the year 2000, to develop by

December 1988 a basin-wide plan for the reduction and control of toxic materials, to develop and

adopt by July 1988 a basin-wide plan for the management and control of pollutants entering the

Bay from point and non-point sources and bottom sediments. There were other commitments and

schedules developed with short timetables and specific actions being required. (3) Population

Growth and Development. Unplanned, uncontrolled growth is tantamount to continuing the Bay's

decline. We agreed to look for ways to mitigate the adverse effects of continued population

growth. That called for the development of guidelines to reduce adverse impacts on the Bay's

water quality and living resources, the creation of a panel of experts to report on anticipated

population growth and land development patterns in the region through the year 2020. That work continues to form the basis for ongoing agreements and legislation. We also agreed to use our resources to educate the public on what's at stake with the Chesapeake Bay. We agreed to develop communications plans, education and information programs, and to look for ways to increase the availability of public access to the waters and shores of the Bay. • In effect, the agreement put the jurisdictions on a "fast track" schedule to develop the information and to build a consensus required to advance legislation, to increase funding, and push for increased enforcement actions. While the agreement set forth some 29 commitments, by 1990, the jurisdictions had met in a timely way 26 of those commitments and the remainder were on track. Significant legislative actions were taken in the various states to deal with land use matters, agencies were established or reorganized, phosphate detergents were banned, and use of the

toxin TBT was severely limited. • The 1987 agreement was important for both policy and process reasons. The agreement and subsequent commitments established a Bay-wide monitoring plan and provided for technical assistance and research toward better means of monitoring progress toward a more stable Chesapeake Bay. • Why is monitoring so important? Because it prevents waste of precious resources on ineffective measures; helps set priorities among the several problems to be attacked; measures the level of success and, therefore, provides political ammunition for further appropriations. • Without credible information showing how the long-term environmental and economic costs of ignoring the Bay exceed the short-term economic costs, passage of legislation and appropriations needed to support the agreement will face much tougher opposition. • The regional scope of many policy issues affecting the Chesapeake also complicates attempts to address them, and the Chesapeake offers an excellent example of such a

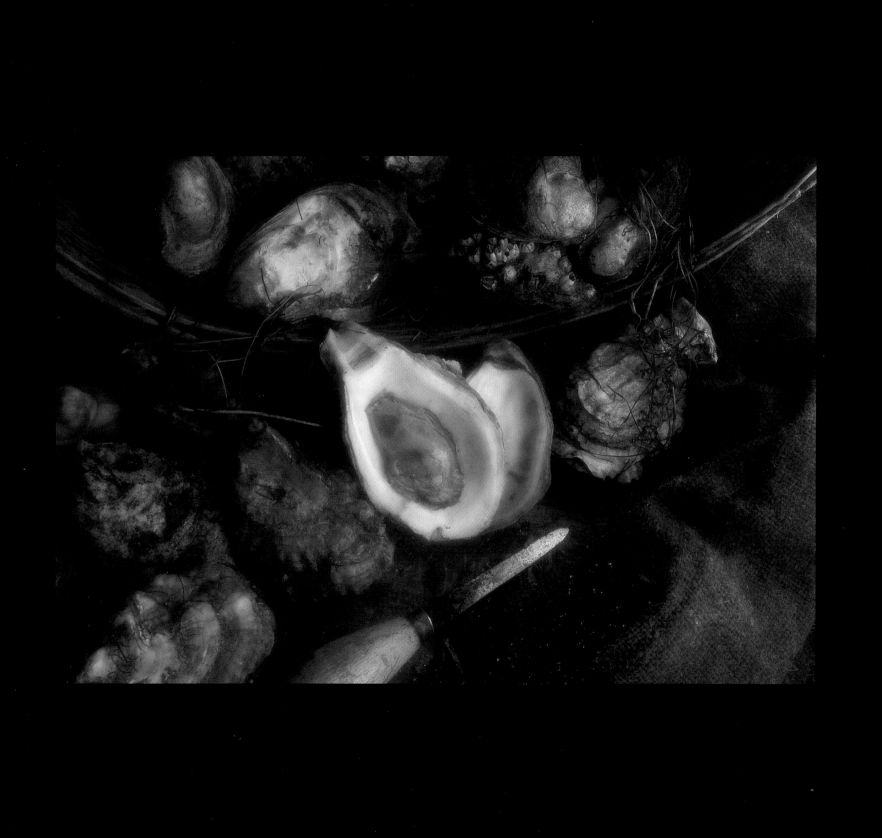

situation. The sheer size of the watershed means the governments of hundreds of localities, several states, and the federal government must cooperate. Herding cats is easier. But without cooperation, dumping in one area might eliminate the gains produced by another locality's strict pollution controls. • Furthermore, cooperation must be ensured over time. A clean Bay requires a commitment for the long haul. Long-term is a problem phrase in government. Government, like most human activities, is usually rooted in the present. The time horizons of those in government are sometimes limited to the next budget cycle, the next legislative cycle, or the next election cycle. • The Chesapeake has suffered from decades of neglect. Even the most able, energetic effort could not hope for complete success within the single four-year term to which the Virginia Constitution limited me. So, from my perspective any effective plan to restore the Bay had to ensure cooperation and outlast the terms of those who signed. • The public nature of the 1987

agreement provided mutual assurances that commitments would be met. And the agreement

offered specific and precise numbers and dates for many of the commitments. Beyond all these

troubles, clean-up efforts confronted a problem of implementation and enforcement. The signers

couldn't carry out the agreement alone. Imagine a clean-up effort without the cooperation of

state agencies in each state. • Likewise, Governor Schaefer and I could not have spent all our

hours looking over the shoulders of the state groups charged with carrying out the specifics of our

agreement. But careless or vague instructions often fail to achieve the desired effect. Especially

when they are interpreted by the agencies of several different states simultaneously. • Therefore,

these commitments and the plans to enact them had to be constructed in a manner that ensured

their intent, and not just their words, would be met by all parties. The problem of confused or

inconsistent enforcement particularly affected the area of land management. • Most decisions involving land use take place through the zoning decisions of local governments. Without

consistency, development in Baltimore County, Maryland, or Arlington County, Virginia, might

undo the gains made by Prince George's County or Prince William County. The agreement signed

in 1987 focused on these issues of cooperation and sustainability in particular. Rather than create

a single program, the agreement produced an ongoing process, a process designed to build upon

itself. • At the root of any sustained, effective government program is public support.

• Involved citizens ensure that legislators — and governors — will continue to focus on an issue,

despite changes in the officeholders. To encourage involvement and interest, the Chesapeake Bay

Agreement required a coordinated, comprehensive communication plan to help spread the word

that *everybody* has a stake in the Bay and its future. By selling environmental programs in terms

of their importance to economic development, transportation, or health, leaders can also ease the

sharpness of apparent trade-offs. • Success not only requires involvement and energy from the

public at large, the particular people enforcing and implementing the programs must be co-opted.

Their employees outlast most legislators, governors, and many judges. If their enthusiasm on an

issue can be assured, especially across agency boundaries, sustainability will be much easier. • So

to offer them a stake in the programs and policies resulting from the 1987 agreement, it called for

their heavy involvement in the specific proposals produced as a result of the agreement. State

agency heads would have had difficulty opposing a plan they helped design. • We, the signers,

realized that the wider range of people we involved, the greater chance for ultimate success

existed. And the agreement's strategies have met with some success. Since Maryland, Virginia,

and the District of Columbia banned phosphates in cleaning products to help achieve the goal of a

40% reduction, the level of phosphates entering the Bay has declined dramatically. If we maintain

Our momentum, we can easily reach our target phosphate levels for the year 2000. To reach our

goal, we need similar efforts on the tributaries of the Bay. • During my own administration

Virginia instituted a best-management practices (BMP) program to encourage practices that

limited runoff and soil erosion. The results were almost immediately apparent. After signing over

1,000 farmers into the program, benefiting over 55,000 acres in the watershed, phosphate runoff

dropped by 1.8 million pounds. The program also prevented the erosion of over 320,000 tons of

soil. • Other jurisdictions have taken similar steps with significant results. This shows the power

of grass-roots efforts to enact sustained and visible change. Other signs of progress can be found

in land use controls adopted by the legislatures of Maryland and Virginia, for example; reductions

have been made in point and non-point sources of pollution entering the Bay, greater

enforcement actions have been taken, greater understanding has been promoted among the

public about the problems facing the Bay, and the policies and programs designed to help it and to foster individual responsibility and stewardship of the Bay's resources. • Legislative support increased across the board. For example, my last Virginia budget, 1988-90, approved by the General Assembly, invested more than $230 million to improve air and water quality, to enhance outdoor recreation, to protect fish and game resources, to advance the handling of solid waste, and to preserve natural and historic assets. The amount allocated to clean up the Chesapeake Bay alone, nearly $55 million, represented more than a 22% increase over Bay funding during the previous two years. • Perhaps the most important progress made during the past decade has been the development of political and public understanding and support of the Bay. The most recent agreements build on that public understanding and support. • The history of the past decade shows the development of a long-term, comprehensive effort to restore the Bay, its tributaries and the living resources of that vast rich body of water. The length and detail of those agreements reflect the increasing public commitment to this important responsibility. • The approach to the restoration of the Bay has several unique qualities that are essential to success. First, it is a regional approach. This is important since the Bay is a complex natural system that ignores political boundaries. Second, it is an inter-governmental approach. Success can be achieved only if all governments with jurisdiction over the lands and waters of the Bay region are full partners in the healing process. Third, it is an approach that strives for consensus and cooperation derived from a common desire to improve the quality of life for all who depend on the Bay. Finally, it is a public approach. We must insist on high standards of program evaluation and accountability because otherwise public support wanes. Without active public participation in the process, progress is threatened. • While achievements over the last decade have been

substantial — so are the challenges that remain. The Bay's condition symbolizes an increasing

paradox and dilemma of American public policy making. • By all accounts the public wants

economic growth or at least the public wants the products of economic growth — meaning

increased opportunity, more jobs for individuals, more income for families, greater prosperity.

• But the public often does not understand the cost — a cost measured in lost rural lands, impure

air and water, and damaged and declining natural resources — a cost also measured in the

enormous sums of public and private funds required to clean up the Bay, whether the economy is

booming or in a state of decline. • Indeed, resource protection has escalated into one of the

highest, broadest and most compelling public concerns in the country. Which again is not to say

Americans are willing to jettison their economic future. Thus, the contradiction. The paradox.

Ambivalence is one of the hazards of a democracy. But it cannot be an excuse for inaction.

those charged with making policy must not falter in the face of complexity. In the case of the Chesapeake Bay, the damage is real and it must be stopped. The Bay must be restored. • But it must be done in a manner that draws people together, rather than driving them apart. That's why the process of creating the Chesapeake Bay agreements over the last decade are so important: the level of concern has been raised, consensus for action has been created and the level of debate has been elevated. It must be sustained. • But we cannot sit back and bask in past successes. Sustained progress toward a better Bay is incremental, and will require continued vigilance from you, the inheritors of the Chesapeake Bay. • Let lessons learned from the fight for a healthier Chesapeake lead to new solutions in other fields of concern as well. • If you are convinced you have a stake in the Bay — and you should by now — it will continue to demand your attention. • In the process of doing so, you will do more than improve the Chesapeake Bay. You will ensure its future

is solely dedicated to the support of the state's natural history museum. In doing so, the foundation embrac
reserve and interpret Virginia's natural heritage in ways that are relevant to all the citizens of the Commonw
um without walls" extends into virtually every corner of the state to promote scientific literacy through rese
ibits and publications. Through these outreach efforts, the museum serves, informs and enriches more than
scientific curators, in addition to their research, lead discovery expeditions to scientific points of interest. Th
ing the Baliles administration.

ation

more than 80,000, the foundation is the largest nonprofit conservation organization working to "save the Bay
ns, corporations and its membership. It has more than 120 staff members spread throughout Virginia, Mary
areas are: environmental education, which reaches more than 35,000 students and their teachers annually; e
s and lawyers who advise decision-makers and offer specific recommendations to protect water quality and
otect wildlife habitat, forest and agricultural land in the watershed. The foundation is the recipient of the Pr
enge Award, the nation's highest environmental honor, and the National Geographic Society Chairman's A

his book are copyrighted by John Hurt Whitehead III. All paintings in this book are copyrighted b

ously contributed six images of paintings from his remarkable Chesapeake Bay art. They are, in o

" Rappahannock River crab potters

Crabbing on Dymer Creek